Table of Contents

Introduction to CSS

Cascading Style Sheets (CSS) is a vital technology in the realm of web development that plays a crucial role in determining how web pages look and are presented to users. Unlike HTML, which focuses on structuring content, CSS is all about presentation and styling.

Imagine a web page without any styling - just plain text and content. That's where CSS steps in. It empowers you to transform the raw content into visually appealing and organized layouts. From choosing the right font styles and sizes to deciding on colors, spacing, and positioning, CSS provides the tools to create engaging and user-friendly designs.

Why CSS Matters

1. **Visual Appeal:** CSS enables you to create eye-catching designs that capture users' attention and make your website stand out.

2. **Consistency:** By centralizing style rules, CSS promotes uniformity across your website. This ensures that fonts, colors, and layouts remain consistent from one

page to another, contributing to a cohesive user experience.

3. **Separation of Concerns:** One of CSS's key strengths is its ability to separate content from presentation. This means you can alter the look of your website without changing the underlying structure of your content. This separation enhances maintainability and makes collaboration between developers and designers smoother.

4. **Flexibility:** CSS allows you to adapt your website's appearance for different devices and screen sizes. This is critical for delivering a responsive and user-friendly experience on both desktop and mobile devices.

How CSS Works

CSS operates on a system of **selectors** and **declarations**. A **selector** specifies which HTML elements you want to style, while a declaration defines the styling properties you want to apply to those elements.

For instance, you might use CSS to say: "Select all the **<h1>** elements and make their text color blue and the font size 24px."

```css
h1 {
  color: blue;
  font-size: 24px;
}
```

In Summary

CSS is the artist's palette of the web world. It takes the raw materials of HTML and transforms them into visually captivating experiences. By mastering CSS, you gain the power to mold the appearance of your websites and provide users with an engaging and consistent journey through your content. So, let's dive into the world of CSS and unleash your creativity!

Including CSS in Your HTML

When it comes to infusing style into your HTML documents, **Cascading Style Sheets (CSS)** offers you several methods. These methods grant you the power to control the visual appeal of your web pages. Let's explore the three primary ways of including CSS in your HTML.

1. Inline Styling

Inline styling is the quickest way to apply styles directly to individual HTML elements. This method involves using the **style** attribute within the opening tag of an element.

<p style="color: blue; font-size: 16px;">This is a blue and larger font text.</p>

While inline styling is convenient, it's best reserved for small-scale adjustments due to its limited reusability and maintainability.

2. Internal Styling

Internal styling involves embedding CSS rules directly within the **<style>** tags in the **<head>** section of your HTML document. This method is more organized than inline styling and offers greater flexibility.

```html
<!DOCTYPE html>
<html>
<head>
  <style>
    p {
      color: green;
      font-size: 18px;
    }
  </style>
</head>
<body>
  <p>This text is styled using internal CSS.</p>
</body>
</html>
```

Internal styling is ideal for small to medium-sized projects where you want to keep your CSS close to your HTML, but it may become unwieldy for larger projects.

3. External Styling

External styling is the gold standard for managing CSS in larger projects. This method involves creating a separate

.css file and linking it to your HTML document using the **<link>** element within the **<head>** section.

styles.css:

```css
/* styles.css */
p {
  color: purple;
  font-size: 20px;
}
```

index.html:

```html
html

<!DOCTYPE html>
<html>
<head>
  <link rel="stylesheet" type="text/css" href="styles.css">
</head>
<body>
  <p>This text is styled using an external CSS file.</p>
</body>
</html>
```

External styling promotes code modularity, reusability, and maintainability by keeping your HTML and CSS separate. This separation makes collaboration between developers and designers smoother and facilitates updates and changes.

Conclusion

Whether you choose inline, internal, or external styling, each method has its place in the toolbox of a web developer. Depending on the size and complexity of your project, you can select the approach that best suits your needs. Regardless of your choice, the goal remains the same: to make your web pages visually appealing and engaging through the magic of CSS.

CSS Syntax: Creating Style Rules

Cascading Style Sheets (CSS) is all about crafting rules that transform the appearance of your HTML elements. These rules are the building blocks of web design, allowing you to shape your content's presentation. Let's delve into the syntax of CSS and how it enables you to weave your creative magic.

The Anatomy of a Rule

A CSS rule is a set of instructions that govern the style of one or more HTML elements. It comprises two essential components: the **selector** and one or more **declarations**.

1. Selector

The selector specifies which HTML elements the rule applies to. It's like a painter choosing a canvas. Selectors can target specific elements, classes, IDs, or even elements with particular attributes.

```css
css                                              Copy code

/* Selector Example */
h1 {
  /* Declarations will go here */
}
```

2. Declarations

Declarations are enclosed within curly braces **{}** and contain one or more **property-value pairs**. These pairs define the styling properties you want to apply to the selected elements.

```css
/* Declaration Example */
h1 {
  color: blue; /* Property: Value */
  font-size: 24px;
}
```

You can include multiple declarations within the same selector, each separated by a semicolon.

```css
/* Multiple Declarations Example */
p {
  color: green;
  font-size: 16px;
  line-height: 1.5;
}
```

Selectors and Properties in CSS

In the world of Cascading Style Sheets (CSS), selectors and properties are the architects of visual transformation. They work together to give life and character to your HTML elements. Let's explore how selectors pinpoint the elements you want to style, and how properties shape their appearance.

Selectors: Precision Targeting

Selectors are like the eyes of CSS – they focus on specific elements you wish to style. They can target HTML elements, classes, IDs, attributes, and even more complex structures. Selectors provide the framework for your creative palette.

Element Selector

Selects all instances of a specific HTML element.

```css
/* Element Selector Example */
p {
  /* Properties will be applied to all <p> elements */
}
```

Class Selector

Targets elements with a specific class attribute.

```css
/* Class Selector Example */
.button {
  /* Properties for elements with class="button" */
}
```

ID Selector

Targets a single element with a unique ID attribute.

```css
/* ID Selector Example */
#header {
  /* Properties for the element with id="header" */
}
```

Universal Selector

Targets all elements on the page.

```css
/* Universal Selector Example */
* {
  /* Properties applied to all elements */
}
```

concepts, you're equipped to embark on a journey of crafting visually stunning web designs that captivate and engage your audience. So, pick your selectors, choose your properties, and let your creativity flow!

CSS Box Model: Building Blocks of Layout Design

In the world of Cascading Style Sheets (CSS), every element is like a puzzle piece within a rectangular box. This concept is known as the box model, and it's a cornerstone of layout design. Understanding the box model is essential for creating well-structured and visually pleasing web layouts.

The Components of the Box Model

Each HTML element is encased within four layers that make up the box model: **content**, **padding**, **border**, and **margin.**

1. **Content**: This is the innermost layer where your actual content resides. It includes text, images, or other HTML elements.

2. **Padding**: Surrounding the content, the padding is a transparent space between the content and the border. It helps create breathing room around the content.

3. **Border**: The border forms a visible boundary around the element. It can be customized in terms of color, style, and thickness.

4. **Margin**: The outermost layer, the margin, is a transparent space between the element and adjacent elements. It helps control the spacing between elements.

Box Model in CSS

In CSS, you can control each aspect of the box model using corresponding properties. Here's a quick overview:

width and **height**: Determine the dimensions of the content area.

padding: Creates space between the content and the border.

border: Defines the border properties like color, style, and thickness.

margin: Sets the space outside the element, affecting its positioning in the layout.

```css
/* Box Model Properties Example */
.box {
  width: 200px;
  height: 150px;
  padding: 20px;
  border: 2px solid #333;
  margin: 10px;
}
```

Box Sizing

By default, the **width** and **height** properties control the dimensions of the content area. However, you can alter this behavior using the **box-sizing** property. When set to **border-box**, it includes padding and border within the defined dimensions.

```css
/* Box Sizing Example */
.box {
  width: 200px;
  height: 150px;
  padding: 20px;
  border: 2px solid #333;
  box-sizing: border-box;
}
```

Conclusion

The CSS box model is like a container that encapsulates your content, giving you control over its presentation and spacing. Mastering the box model equips you with the ability to create clean and organized layouts, ensuring that your web pages look and feel just the way you envision. So remember, every element is a box, and understanding how to manipulate that box is the key to layout success!

Working with Text in CSS: Typography Mastery

When it comes to web design, Cascading Style Sheets (CSS) opens up a world of possibilities for crafting captivating typography. From choosing the perfect typefaces to adjusting line heights, CSS gives you the power to make text not only readable but also visually appealing. Let's dive into the art of working with text in CSS.

1. **Font Family**
   The **font-family** property lets you specify the typeface for your text. You can list multiple fonts in case the user's preferred font is not available.

```css
/* Font Family Example */
body {
  font-family: "Helvetica Neue", Arial, sans-serif;
}
```

2. Font Size

With the **font-size** property, you can determine the size of your text. You can use various units, such as pixels, ems, or percentages.

```css
css                                              Copy code

/* Font Size Example */
h1 {
    font-size: 36px;
}
p {
    font-size: 18px;
}
```

3. Text Align

The **text-align** property controls the alignment of text within its containing element. It can be set to **left**, **center**, **right**, or **justify**.

```css
css                                              Copy code

/* Text Align Example */
h1 {
    text-align: center;
}
```

4. Line Height

The **line-height** property defines the space between lines of text. It's crucial for readability and aesthetics.

```css
/* Line Height Example */
p {
    line-height: 1.5;
}
```

5. Font Weight

The **font-weight** property allows you to set the thickness of the text. Common values are **normal**, **bold**, and numeric values like **400** or **700.**

```css
/* Font Weight Example */
strong {
    font-weight: bold;
}
```

6. Text Decoration

Use the **text-decoration** property to add or remove text decorations like underlines, overlines, and line-through.

```css
/* Text Decoration Example */
a {
    text-decoration: none; /* Remove underlines from links */
}
```

7. Text Transform

The **text-transform** property lets you control the capitalization of text, making it uppercase, lowercase, or capitalized.

```css
/* Text Transform Example */
h2 {
    text-transform: uppercase;
}
```

8. Font Style

The **font-style** property allows you to italicize or oblique the text.

```css
/* Font Style Example */
em {
    font-style: italic;
}
```

9. Letter Spacing

The **letter-spacing** property adds space between characters, which can be used for both decorative and readability purposes.

```css
/* Letter Spacing Example */
h3 {
    letter-spacing: 2px;
}
```

10. **Color**

Set the **color** of your text using the color property.

```css
/* Color Example */
p {
  color: #333; /* Hexadecimal color value */
}
```

Conclusion

Typography is the soul of design, and CSS empowers you to mold your text into a visual masterpiece. By skillfully manipulating properties like font-family, font-size, and more, you can create an immersive reading experience that complements your overall design vision. So, experiment with these text-related properties and watch as your content comes to life with typography magic!

Styling Links in CSS: Unveiling Interactive Elegance

Hyperlinks, the bridges that connect web pages, are essential for navigation. But why settle for plain links when you can elevate them with stunning visual effects? With **Cascading Style Sheets (CSS)**, you can transform links using pseudo-classes, giving users an engaging and interactive experience. Let's explore how to style links in different states.

1. :link and :visited

The **:link** pseudo-class targets unvisited links, while **:visited** targets links that have been clicked by users. You can modify their appearance to differentiate between the two states.

```css
css                                    Copy code

/* Styling Unvisited and Visited Links */
a:link {
  color: blue; /* Unvisited link color */
  text-decoration: underline;
}


a:visited {
  color: purple; /* Visited link color */
}
```

2. :hover

The **:hover** pseudo-class is activated when a user hovers their cursor over a link. It's an excellent opportunity to provide visual feedback to users.

```css
css                                    Copy code

/* Styling Hovered Links */
a:hover {
  color: red; /* Color change on hover */
  text-decoration: none; /* Remove underline on hover */
}
```

3. :active

When a user clicks on a link, the **:active** pseudo-class takes effect. It's a momentary state that can be used to give a click interaction visual feedback.

```css
/* Styling Active Links */
a:active {
  color: green; /* Color change when clicked */
}
```

Example

```css
/* Link Styling Example */
a:link {
  color: blue;
  text-decoration: underline;
}


a:visited {
  color: purple;
}


a:hover {
  color: red;
  text-decoration: none;
}


a:active {
  color: green;
}
```

Conclusion

Links are the navigational arteries of the web, and styling them enhances user experience and aesthetics. By harnessing the power of pseudo-classes like :link, :visited, :hover, and :active, you can create a seamless and visually engaging journey for your users. So, go ahead and let your creativity flow as you infuse life into your links with CSS magic!

Adding Colors and Backgrounds in CSS: Painting Your Canvas

Colors and backgrounds are the paintbrushes of the web designer's palette. **Cascading Style Sheets (CSS)** empowers you to infuse life into your elements with a vivid array of colors and captivating backgrounds. Let's explore how you can bring your designs to life by mastering color and background properties.

1. Color Properties

You can set colors using various methods, including color names, hexadecimal codes, RGB values, and more.

Using Color Names

```css
/* Using Color Names */
h1 {
  color: red;
}
```

Using Hexadecimal Codes

```css
CSS

/* Using Hexadecimal Codes */
p {
  color: #3498db;
}
```

Using RGB Values

```css
CSS

/* Using RGB Values */
a {
  color: rgb(255, 0, 0);
}
```

2. Background Color

The **background-color** property lets you set the background color of an element.

```css
CSS

/* Background Color Example */
button {
  background-color: #f39c12;
}
```

3. Background Image

You can set background images using the **background-image** property. This can be a local or external image file.

```css
/* Background Image Example */
header {
  background-image: url("header-bg.jpg");
  background-size: cover; /* Adjust background image size */
}
```

4. Background Repeat and Position

You can control how background images repeat using **background-repeat** and adjust their starting position using **background-position**.

```css
/* Background Repeat and Position Example */
section {
  background-image: url("pattern-bg.png");
  background-repeat: repeat-x; /* Repeat only horizontally */
  background-position: center top; /* Position at the top center */
}
```

5. Background Shorthand

The **background** shorthand property allows you to set multiple background-related properties in one line.

```css
/* Background Shorthand Example */
div {
  background: url("bg-image.jpg") center/cover no-repeat #333;
}
```

Example

```css
/* Colors and Backgrounds Example */
h2 {
  color: #e74c3c;
  background-color: #f2f2f2;
  padding: 10px;
}

.button {
  background-color: #2ecc71;
  color: white;
  padding: 8px 16px;
}

.box {
  background-image: url("box-bg.jpg");
  background-size: contain;
  background-repeat: no-repeat;
  padding: 20px;
}
```

Conclusion

Colors and backgrounds are the tools that allow you to paint your web canvas with personality and flair. Whether it's using color properties, setting background colors, or creating visually captivating background images, CSS enables you to make a bold statement and leave a lasting impression on your users. So, pick your colors, design your backgrounds, and watch your website come to life!

Positioning Elements in CSS: Crafting Layout Harmony

Positioning elements on a web page is like arranging pieces on a chessboard. **Cascading Style Sheets (CSS)** equips you with a range of strategies to position elements exactly where you want them. Let's explore the various positioning techniques CSS offers to achieve layout harmony.

1. Relative Positioning

With position: relative;, you can shift an element's position relative to its default position. It's often used in combination with top, right, bottom, and left properties.

```css
/* Relative Positioning Example */
.box {
  position: relative;
  top: 20px;
  left: 30px;
}
```

2. Absolute Positioning

The position: absolute; property allows an element to be positioned relative to its nearest positioned ancestor (or the window if there's none). It's perfect for creating overlays or positioning elements precisely.

```css
/* Absolute Positioning Example */
.overlay {
  position: absolute;
  top: 0;
  right: 0;
}
```

3. Fixed Positioning

position: fixed; locks an element's position to the viewport, making it stay fixed even when the user scrolls. It's often used for things like navigation menus.

```css
/* Fixed Positioning Example */
.navbar {
  position: fixed;
  top: 0;
  width: 100%;
}
```

4. Float

The float property is used to make an element float to the left or right within its containing element. This technique is often used for creating layouts with multiple columns.

```css
/* Float Example */
.column {
  float: left;
  width: 50%;
}
```

5. Clear

When using the float property, you might need to clear elements to prevent unwanted wrapping. The clear property ensures an element doesn't float beside previous floated elements.

```css
/* Clear Example */
.clearfix::after {
  content: "";
  display: table;
  clear: both;
}
```

Example

```css
/* Positioning Elements Example */
.header {
  position: fixed;
  top: 0;
  left: 0;
  width: 100%;
  background-color: #333;
  color: white;
  padding: 10px;
}


.sidebar {
  float: left;
  width: 30%;
  background-color: #f2f2f2;
  padding: 20px;
}


.main-content {
  float: left;
  width: 70%;
  padding: 20px;
}
```

Conclusion

Positioning elements is like choreographing a dance on your web canvas. Whether you're shifting elements slightly with relative positioning, giving them precise coordinates with absolute positioning, keeping them fixed with fixed positioning, or creating column layouts with floats, CSS offers the tools you need to create intricate and stunning layouts. So, position your elements strategically and watch your web design masterpiece come to life!

Responsive Design in CSS: Crafting Adaptable Layouts

In a world where devices come in all shapes and sizes, your web design needs to be adaptable. Cascading Style Sheets (CSS) empowers you to create responsive layouts that gracefully adjust to different screen sizes. With the magic of media queries, you can ensure your website looks and functions beautifully across various devices. Let's dive into the art of responsive design.

1. Media Queries

Media queries are the heart of responsive design. They allow you to apply different styles based on the device's characteristics, such as screen width, height, and orientation.

```css
/* Media Query Example */
@media (max-width: 768px) {
  /* Styles for screens up to 768px wide */
  .sidebar {
    display: none; /* Hide sidebar on small screens */
  }
}
```

2. Fluid Layouts

Creating a fluid layout involves using relative units like percentages for widths and ems for fonts. This ensures that elements resize proportionally based on the screen size.

```css
/* Fluid Layout Example */
.container {
  width: 90%; /* Relative width */
  max-width: 1200px; /* Set a maximum width for larger screens */
}

h1 {
  font-size: 2em; /* Relative font size */
}
```

3. Flexbox and Grid

CSS flexbox and grid layouts are powerful tools for creating flexible and responsive designs. They allow you to build complex layouts that adapt to various screen sizes.

```css
/* Flexbox Example */
.container {
  display: flex;
  flex-direction: row; /* Horizontal layout on larger screens */
}

/* Grid Example */
.container {
  display: grid;
  grid-template-columns: 1fr 2fr; /* Two columns on larger screens */
}
```

4. Mobile-First Approach

Embracing a mobile-first approach means designing for mobile devices first and then enhancing the design for larger screens using media queries.

```css
/* Mobile-First Example */
.container {
  padding: 10px;
}

@media (min-width: 768px) {
  .container {
    padding: 20px; /* Increase padding on larger screens */
  }
}
```

Example

```css
/* Responsive Design Example */
.container {
  width: 90%;
  max-width: 1200px;
  margin: 0 auto;
  padding: 20px;
}

@media (max-width: 768px) {
  /* Styles for screens up to 768px wide */
  .container {
    padding: 10px; /* Smaller padding on small screens */
  }
}
```

Conclusion

Responsive design is the art of creating adaptable web experiences that cater to users across various devices. With media queries, fluid layouts, flexbox, grid, and a mobile-first mindset, CSS empowers you to build layouts that seamlessly adjust and provide a delightful user experience, regardless of screen size. So, embrace responsive design and watch your website shine on every device!

CSS Frameworks: Empowering Rapid Web Development

In the fast-paced world of web development, CSS frameworks have emerged as invaluable tools that accelerate the process of building stylish and responsive websites. These frameworks provide a collection of pre-designed CSS components, layout systems, and JavaScript plugins that streamline development and ensure consistency. One of the most popular and widely used CSS frameworks is Bootstrap. Let's explore how CSS frameworks like Bootstrap can supercharge your development process.

1. Introduction to Bootstrap

Bootstrap, developed by Twitter, is an open-source CSS framework that simplifies the creation of modern and responsive web interfaces. It offers a range of pre-styled components, such as navigation bars, buttons, forms, modals, and more. Bootstrap also includes a responsive grid system that makes arranging elements across different screen sizes a breeze.

2. Key Features of Bootstrap

Responsive Grid System

Bootstrap's grid system uses a 12-column layout, allowing you to create responsive designs that adapt to various screen sizes. It's based on a mobile-first approach, making it easy to build websites that work well on smartphones, tablets, and desktops.

Pre-Styled Components

Bootstrap comes with a plethora of pre-designed UI components that can be easily integrated into your project. These components include buttons, forms, navigation bars, alerts, modals, carousels, and more. By using these ready-made components, you save time and ensure a consistent design across your website.

Typography and Utility Classes

Bootstrap provides a variety of typography styles and utility classes that enable you to control spacing, alignment, and other design aspects without writing custom CSS.

JavaScript Plugins

Bootstrap includes a set of JavaScript plugins that enhance the functionality of your website. Examples include dropdown menus, tooltips, modals, and carousels. These plugins can be easily integrated into your project without the need for extensive JavaScript coding.

3. Getting Started with Bootstrap

To get started with Bootstrap, you typically need to include its CSS and JavaScript files in your HTML document. You can either download Bootstrap and host the files yourself or use a content delivery network (CDN) to link to the files hosted on a server.

Here's a basic example of including Bootstrap using a CDN:

```html
<!DOCTYPE html>

<html>

<head>

  <link rel="stylesheet"
href="https://maxcdn.bootstrapcdn.com/bootstrap/4.5.2/css/bootstrap.min.css">

  <script
src="https://ajax.googleapis.com/ajax/libs/jquery/3.5.1/jquery.min.js"></script>

  <script
src="https://maxcdn.bootstrapcdn.com/bootstrap/4.5.2/js/bootstrap.min.js"></script>

</head>

<body>


<!-- Your Bootstrap components and content here -->


</body>

</html>
```

4. Customization and Theming

While Bootstrap offers a default look and feel, you can customize it to match your brand's identity. Bootstrap provides theming options that allow you to change colors, fonts, and other design elements to create a unique appearance.

Conclusion

CSS frameworks like Bootstrap have revolutionized web development by providing developers with a toolkit of pre-designed components and layouts. They significantly speed up development time, ensure a consistent and professional design, and facilitate responsive layouts that adapt seamlessly to different devices. By integrating Bootstrap into your projects, you empower yourself to create beautiful and functional websites efficiently. So, explore the world of CSS frameworks, unleash your creativity, and watch your web development journey soar to new heights!

Debugging CSS with Browser Developer Tools: Unveiling the Mysteries

Web development is a creative journey, but it's not without its challenges. Sometimes, your CSS might not behave the way you intended, leading to styling issues that need to be resolved. Enter browser developer tools, your trusty companions for inspecting, debugging, and fine-tuning your CSS code in real-time. Let's embark on a journey to uncover the secrets of debugging CSS using these powerful tools.

1. Accessing Developer Tools

Most modern web browsers come equipped with developer tools that can be accessed by right-clicking on an element and selecting "Inspect" or by pressing F12 or Ctrl + Shift + I (Windows/Linux) or Cmd + Option + I (Mac). This opens a panel where you can explore the HTML structure and associated CSS rules.

2. Inspecting Elements

The Elements tab in developer tools displays the HTML structure of the page. By hovering over or clicking on elements, you can visualize their dimensions, margins, paddings, and borders in the viewport. It helps you identify how the layout is structured and where potential styling issues might arise.

3. Viewing and Modifying CSS

The Styles tab reveals the applied CSS rules for the selected element. You can see which rules are being applied, overridden, or inherited. By modifying these rules in real-time, you can experiment with different styles to pinpoint the source of a problem.

4. Identifying Selectors and Properties

Developer tools help you understand the specificity of CSS selectors and properties. You can hover over a CSS property to see which rule defined it and what values it's inheriting.

5. Debugging Issues

When you encounter unexpected styling behavior, you can utilize the following debugging techniques:

a. Disable or Modify Rules

Temporarily disable or modify CSS rules to see if the issue persists or changes. This helps you isolate problematic styles.

b. Use Pseudo-Classes

Utilize pseudo-classes like :hover or :active to inspect how elements behave in different states.

c. Check Box Model

Inspect padding, margins, and borders to ensure they're contributing to the layout as intended.

d. Debug Responsiveness

Use the responsive design mode in developer tools to test how your website appears on different screen sizes.

6. Console and Logs

The Console tab can be used to log messages, errors, and JavaScript interactions. This is invaluable for debugging scripts that interact with your CSS.

7. Network Tab

The Network tab shows all resources loaded by the webpage, including CSS files. It can help you identify issues with loading stylesheets.

8. Examine Box Model

The Box Model view in developer tools visually represents an element's dimensions, padding, borders, and margins. This can help you identify layout issues.

Conclusion

Browser developer tools are your ally in unraveling the mysteries of CSS glitches and layout conundrums. They empower you to inspect, diagnose, and experiment with your CSS code in real-time, giving you the insights you need to resolve styling issues efficiently. By mastering these tools, you'll become a debugging ninja, ensuring that your web designs shine flawlessly on any screen. So, dive into the world of developer tools and conquer the challenges that lie ahead!

Resources for Further Learning: Embarking on Your CSS Journey

Congratulations on embarking on your journey to master Cascading Style Sheets (CSS)! As you delve into the world of web design and styling, you'll find a plethora of resources that can help you navigate the complexities of CSS with confidence. Here's a curated list of resources that will serve as your compass on this exciting learning adventure:

1. MDN Web Docs (developer.mozilla.org)

The MDN Web Docs offer comprehensive and authoritative documentation on HTML, CSS, JavaScript, and various web technologies. The CSS section covers everything from basic concepts to advanced topics, making it an invaluable resource for learners at all levels.

2. Codecademy (codecademy.com)

Codecademy provides interactive and hands-on tutorials that guide you through the process of learning CSS. You'll find courses tailored to beginners, as well as more advanced topics like responsive design and flexbox.

3. freeCodeCamp (freecodecamp.org)

freeCodeCamp is a community-driven platform that offers coding challenges, projects, and tutorials. Their curriculum includes a comprehensive CSS section that covers key concepts and real-world projects.

4. CSS-Tricks (css-tricks.com)

CSS-Tricks is a treasure trove of tutorials, guides, and articles focused on CSS and front-end web development. It covers a wide range of topics, from foundational concepts to cutting-edge techniques.

5. W3Schools (w3schools.com)

W3Schools is known for its beginner-friendly tutorials and examples for web development technologies, including CSS. It's a great starting point for those new to CSS.

6. CSS Zen Garden (csszengarden.com)

CSS Zen Garden is a unique platform that showcases the creative possibilities of CSS. It demonstrates how the same HTML can be transformed into visually stunning designs using only CSS.

Next Steps in Your CSS Journey: From Learning to Mastery

Congratulations on completing the beginner's guide to CSS! You've taken the first steps towards becoming a skilled web designer. As you continue your journey, here are some next steps to help you progress from learning to mastery:

1. Practice, Practice, Practice

Practice is the foundation of mastery. Keep coding and experimenting with CSS on a regular basis. Create personal projects, replicate existing websites, or design your own web pages to apply what you've learned.

2. Build Real Projects

Apply your CSS skills to real-world projects. Start small with simple websites and gradually tackle more complex projects. Building real projects will give you hands-on experience and showcase your abilities to potential employers or clients.

3. Explore Advanced Concepts

Dive deeper into advanced CSS concepts such as flexbox, CSS Grid, animations, transitions, and responsive design techniques. These skills will empower you to create dynamic and engaging user experiences.

4. Learn CSS Preprocessors

Explore CSS preprocessors like Sass or LESS. These tools enhance your CSS workflow by adding features like variables, nesting, and functions, making your code more organized and maintainable.

5. Study Design Principles

A good understanding of design principles is essential for creating visually appealing and user-friendly websites.

Study typography, color theory, layout design, and user experience (UX) principles to enhance your design skills.

6. Stay Updated

Web technologies evolve rapidly. Stay updated with the latest CSS specifications, trends, and best practices. Follow industry blogs, forums, and newsletters to stay informed about the latest developments.

7. Collaborate and Seek Feedback

Collaborate with other developers, designers, and enthusiasts. Participate in online communities, attend local meetups, and share your work for feedback. Constructive feedback can help you identify areas for improvement.

8. Explore Frameworks and Libraries

Explore CSS frameworks like Bootstrap, Foundation, or Tailwind CSS. These frameworks provide reusable components and responsive layouts that can streamline your development process.

9. Master Browser Developer Tools

Become proficient in using browser developer tools for debugging and optimization. Understanding how to diagnose and fix CSS issues will save you time and frustration.

10. Create a Portfolio

As you gain more experience, create a portfolio showcasing your projects. A well-organized portfolio is a powerful tool to demonstrate your skills and attract potential clients or employers.

Conclusion

Your journey with CSS is an ongoing adventure filled with continuous learning and growth. Embrace challenges, seek knowledge, and keep your curiosity alive. Remember that mastery takes time, so be patient with yourself. With dedication and a passion for crafting beautiful and functional web experiences, you're well on your way to becoming a proficient and confident web designer. Keep coding and creating, and let your creativity flourish!